THE GAME
OF LIGHT

Y York

BROADWAY PLAY PUBLISHING INC
New York
www.broadwayplaypublishing.com
info@broadwayplaypublishing.com

THE GAME OF LIGHT
© Copyright 2001 Y York

All rights reserved. This work is fully protected under the copyright laws of the United States of America. No part of this publication may be photocopied, reproduced, stored in a retrieval system, or transmitted, in any form or by any means, electronic, mechanical, recording, or otherwise, without the prior permission of the publisher. Additional copies of this play are available from the publisher.

Written permission is required for live performance of any sort. This includes readings, cuttings, scenes, and excerpts. For amateur and stock performances, please contact Broadway Play Publishing Inc. For all other rights please contact the author c/o B P P I.

First published by B P P I in October 2001 in *Plays By Y York, Volume 2*
This edition: September 2018
I S B N: 978-0-88145-798-8

Book design: Marie Donovan
Page make-up: Adobe InDesign
Typeface: Palatino

THE GAME OF LIGHT was originally commissioned by New City Theater, John Kazanjian, Artistic Director; subsequently workshopped at The New Harmony Project, Andrew Tsau, Artistic Director; and ASK Theatre Projects, Mead K Hunter, Director of Literary Programs (both workshops directed by Veronica Brady); and Blue Heron's Spring Forward Reading Series in N Y C, directed by Leslie Hoban Blake.

Acknowledgments: Many thanks to the actors who participated in the workshops and readings of the play. Special thanks to Demene Hall, John Holyoke, Tracy Leigh, Kim Scott, and Sloan Shelton.

CHARACTERS & SETTING

ANTONY, *a white man from New York City. Also plays* JAMES, *ten*

JANNA, *an African-American woman from New York City. Also plays* ANNIE, *eight*

An office on the 33rd floor. Seattle, 1993.

The objects that appear in the play are present and visible from the beginning of the play. There are no scenery or costume changes or blackouts; there is only the wind. The designation of "scene" is for convenience.

for Korina Layne-Jones

(Scene One. The present. A single room, two-person office. The furniture is timeless and expensive. A closet. The technology [computer, fax] is in the background. A very bad wind storm is underway. JANNA *is on the phone when* ANTONY *rushes in, takes off his coat, hangs it in closet. They are immediately tense.)*

ANTONY: I'm sorry, I'm sorry—

JANNA: Don't worry about it.

ANTONY: There was a tree in the road—

JANNA: The depositions aren't even here yet.

ANTONY: Didn't Laurie send them?

JANNA: I'm trying to find out. Machine. *(Hangs up)*

ANTONY: Did you leave a message?

JANNA: At eight, eight fifteen, and a quarter to nine.

ANTONY: Can we call the messenger service?

JANNA: If she isn't in, she didn't call a messenger.

ANTONY: If I don't have the depositions—

JANNA: I know, Laurie knows, everybody knows—for Pete's sake, Antony.

ANTONY: I'm sorry. Was I pushy?

JANNA: ...Enthusiastic.

ANTONY: I was pushy. I can't help it. Everything—everybody is so slow.

JANNA: They call it laid back.

ANTONY: I told her I'd come get them. Two blocks. It would have been so easy. Why couldn't she have just said, yes, come get them?

JANNA: It would have seemed "pushy".

ANTONY: Boy, this town. Nobody ever gives me a straight answer.

JANNA: There's a city ordinance against a straight answer.

ANTONY: That explains it. When I was looking for an apartment, I saw one, I liked it, I said, when can I move in? "Move in? Oh, we didn't know you'd want to *move in.*" I was speechless. I had answered an *ad* in the *newspaper* for an *apartment*. *(Rhetorical)* What could they possibly have thought I was doing there?

JANNA: Yeah, I thought it was a race thing.

ANTONY: Oh. *(Brief pause)* I didn't even think of that. Maybe you're right, maybe they didn't like me.

JANNA: *(Joking)* Maybe your car isn't fancy enough.

ANTONY: No, my car is fancy enough. My car is embarrassingly fancy.

JANNA: ...I don't know then.

ANTONY: You're not like that. You say what you mean.

JANNA: I'm an ex-New Yorker, too. It's in the blood.

ANTONY: That's so funny—I never thought of myself as a New Yorker.

JANNA: Yeah, the rest of the country never lets you forget it. Antony, your tie.

ANTONY: I'm *what*?

JANNA: Your *tie*, where's your tie? You have court—

ANTONY: Oh! I have it. Right here. *(From pocket)* I ran out so fast—um…

JANNA: And there was a tree in the road.

ANTONY: There *was* a tree in the road.

JANNA: I'm just kidding.

(Brief pause)

ANTONY: I gotta print the files before the hearing.

JANNA: They're in your briefcase.

ANTONY: In my—

JANNA: You were on the phone when I left—

ANTONY: Oh, I—

JANNA: You said you wanted to work last night so I printed the files and put them in your briefcase.

ANTONY: I did work. I make the calls at night because of the time difference. Isn't that how you do it?

JANNA: I don't call. I fax. I don't like to talk to Pakár.

ANTONY: Which one is he?

JANNA: Victims' claims.

ANTONY: He's on our side.

JANNA: Too bad for our side.

ANTONY: No, we're gonna win this. India is strong on the environment.

JANNA: Now if they would just stop setting fire to their wives.

ANTONY: …They have a very progressive environmental policy.

JANNA: Well, that's something I guess.

(Pause. ANTONY takes the printed files from his briefcase. He gets out a tattered old book and a framed photograph. He takes them to a shelf where there are already photos and an old microscope.)

ANTONY: Can I…?

JANNA: …Oh, sure, go ahead.

ANTONY: Just a couple of things.

JANNA: Bring in whatever you like.

ANTONY: No, I just like to keep these around. (Picks up a photograph) These your kids?

JANNA: Yeah. What time is the hearing?

ANTONY: One-thirty.

JANNA: I'll take you through the depositions at lunch—they should be here by then.

ANTONY: Great. How about Wild Basil, my treat.

JANNA: Oh. No. When I go out I never get back on track.

ANTONY: We should go out. Get some daylight.

JANNA: Yeah, in this hurricane, it'll be delightful.

ANTONY: I hate fluorescent lights.

JANNA: (Defensive) I get full-spectrum.

ANTONY: The hallway is so dreary. Sam told me you're pretty sold on this building.

JANNA: It was the best I could do on short notice.

ANTONY: I'll bet we could find a better office.

JANNA: We're not going to be here that long.

ANTONY: It isn't safe.

JANNA: It's safe.

ANTONY: The stairwell doors lock behind you.

JANNA: That's so fleeing robbers get trapped. A "safety feature".

ANTONY: What if there's a fire?

JANNA: I'll call a fire engine.

ANTONY: How are we supposed to get out of the building?

JANNA: We'll take the stairs, like the sign says.

ANTONY: And be locked in.

JANNA: Not at the bottom.

ANTONY: Yes, I checked.

JANNA: Jeez, Antony, talk to Maintenance. If I call now we'll have lunch by lunch time.

ANTONY: They don't have anything I like.

JANNA: It's just lunch. Get soup and a sandwich.

ANTONY: What kind of sandwich?

JANNA: I don't know, tuna fish.

ANTONY: There's a boycott.

JANNA: Get chicken.

ANTONY: They won't be free range. *(Explanation)* Free range. Peck peck in the dirt instead of kept in cages.

JANNA: I know what free range is. I'm gonna get an avocado melt. Do you want one?

ANTONY: B G H. The cheese.

JANNA: What do you care? You've done all your growing.

ANTONY: It's not about growing. It's about cruelty to cows.

JANNA: Crueler than it already is?

ANTONY: Yes, actually. Twenty-five percent crueler.

JANNA: I didn't know we could calibrate cruelty now.

ANTONY: *(Explanation)* They're on the milking machine twenty-five percent longer. They get all these infections and sores on their…. *(Brief pause)* I'm sorry.

JANNA: About what?

ANTONY: I didn't mean to talk about—I'm sorry.

JANNA: *(Brief pause)* Oh my God. You didn't mean to talk about *cow udders* in front of me?

ANTONY: No, I did not.

JANNA: Well, actually, it's okay to talk about cow udders in front of me. I actually didn't think you were making a reference or comparison to me or any other human female and a cow. You didn't mean to do that, did you?

ANTONY: I did not. *(Brief pause)*

JANNA: You shouldn't listen to Fitz, Antony.

ANTONY: No, I know.

JANNA: Not about me.

ANTONY: He helped me out, Janna—

JANNA: He wants an ally.

ANTONY: Well, that may be true—

JANNA: It is true.

ANTONY: He seems like a perfectly nice man.

JANNA: That's because he doesn't come up behind you—

ANTONY: Janna—

JANNA: —and push into your rear end—

ANTONY: Please—

JANNA: —with his penis perfectly erect.

ANTONY: You don't know that! You don't. You can't always tell—he's a big man. He's a big sloppy Irishman with affectionate habits—

JANNA: My God, you're quoting him!

ANTONY: —It's cultural—and sometimes you can't tell—when it accidentally—it just feels like it, but it's a perfectly natural hang—and it's not... what you said. Erect.

JANNA: Believe me, Antony, I don't come from a cold culture.

ANTONY: No, I know, but...he's amazing—we worked side by side on the logging bill—until Sam switched me here—

JANNA: What were you doing with the logging bill?

ANTONY: Fitz wanted me to check some precedents.

JANNA: Why?

ANTONY: To see if they exist.

JANNA: They exist.

ANTONY: I know, I checked.

JANNA: That pig. The logging bill is moot.

ANTONY: No.

JANNA: Yes. If it weren't I wouldn't be working on India.

ANTONY: ...I don't get it.

JANNA: It's my bill.

ANTONY: Your name is not on it.

JANNA: Why am I not surprised? "Check some precedents."

ANTONY: ...I told him how impressive it was, he smiled.

JANNA: Letting you think *he* wrote it. Logging is mine.

ANTONY: I didn't figure you for a tree freak.

JANNA: Fitz can be a tree freak, but I can't be a tree freak?

ANTONY: You can be whatever kind of freak you want to be—I just didn't know.

JANNA: Sam sold me on saving trees. That's how he got me. Didn't he sell you on something?

ANTONY: He just said the magic word.

JANNA: Which word was that?

ANTONY: Fitz.

JANNA: Sam did *not* promise you Fitz.

ANTONY: No, he didn't. Fitz was on the personnel list.

JANNA: Fitz is on borrowed time. He was on borrowed time when you came on.

ANTONY: I know that, Janna. You—you have every reason to be annoyed with him. Your name should be on that bill—

JANNA: Antony! I am not sitting here all by myself in this tiny office because I didn't get credit on some bill.

ANTONY: I know—

JANNA: No, I don't think you know. This isn't about who did what *work*, or some accidental reference to female anatomy, or female *cow* anatomy—

ANTONY: No—

JANNA: It was not an accident.

ANTONY: No, I know. It's just a shame—

JANNA: Yes, it is a shame!

ANTONY: That he has to go. Is a shame.

JANNA: Well, that is not exactly where I would place the shame.

ANTONY: It's just…

JANNA: What?

ANTONY: He gives us credibility.

JANNA: Who says that?

ANTONY: Nobody has to say it; everybody knows it. He'd be making millions in the real world.

JANNA: We'd all be cleaning up in the real world.

ANTONY: He's why I could walk away from my salary.

JANNA: It's a trade-off. You work here you get to make the world nicer. Nobody can call you a selfish little money-grabber. Think of it as giving back to the community.

ANTONY: I was making almost a hundred thousand dollars—

JANNA: Happens to the best of us.

ANTONY: Everybody doesn't give up a hundred thousand dollars, but I could do it because I was going to get Fitz.

JANNA: You sound just like G E, Tony; "I gave up C F Cs, can't I keep my P C Bs?"

ANTONY: And why not give *them* some credit, too?

JANNA: Who?

ANTONY: Corporations are just like people. You have to give them strokes for their good behavior. They did give up C F Cs.

JANNA: Where do I send the thank-you note?

ANTONY: You don't have to be sarcastic.

JANNA: Yes I do. At least for the four or five years it's going to take me to recover from "corporations are like people". Boy, Tony. You should have stayed on Wall Street.

ANTONY: Maybe I should have.

JANNA: Strokes for good behavior, I mean, gag me, boy.

(The sound of a loud crack, a terrifying gust of wind. They are shaken, scared.)

ANTONY: What was that?

JANNA: I believe that was the wind.

ANTONY: Is the window open?

JANNA: The window *doesn't* open.

ANTONY: How did it get in here?

JANNA: I don't know.

ANTONY: Are you alright?

JANNA: ...Just surprised.

(ANTONY *and* JANNA *both look around. Wind hums through the building.*)

ANTONY: Are you sure you don't want me to find us another office?

(JANNA *snorts a little laugh.* ANTONY *looks down at the storm blowing.*)

JANNA: I didn't mean to call you "boy".

ANTONY: What?

JANNA: I called you "boy".

ANTONY: That's okay, just don't call me *Tony*. My father calls me Tony. *(Snorts a laugh)* I sounded like him. I don't even think that way.

JANNA: What way?

ANTONY: The corporate way. God, I sounded just like my father.

(JANNA *looks out window, too.*)

JANNA: The depositions are probably sitting on Laurie's desk. Do you have your key to Pike Street?

ANTONY: Sure.

JANNA: You better get over there. I'll bet nobody went in.

ANTONY: *(Looking)* God, maybe it *is* a hurricane. *(Brief pause)* Let's get outta here. Let's both go.

JANNA: Yeah. *(She changes the answering machine.)* "Hello, you've reached the Pine Street extension office of E D E. It's ten A M Thursday. We're closing due to bad weather." In case my kids call. *(She gets her coat and briefcase.)* Aren't you coming?

ANTONY: I'm going to try Laurie again. I'd hate to get there and find she'd already sent them. Hold the elevator for me.

JANNA: Okay. She exits.)

ANTONY: *(He gets machine)* Damn. *(Listening to message, then)* Hello Sam. This is Antony on Thursday morning. There seems to be a discrepancy— *(Sigh)* Man, we gotta *talk.*

(JANNA reenters.)

JANNA: Is she there?

ANTONY: Machine. What's up?

JANNA: The elevator light is off. I don't think it's running.

ANTONY: What— *(He dashes to the hallway.)*

JANNA: It's not running —Crazy man. *(To phone)* Come on, pick up. *(Machine)* Swell. Hello maintenance. Phil if you get this, and you better get it, some of your tenants are trapped—

(The lights go out. The only light is from the window. Pale daylight)

ANTONY: *(Enters, distracted)* Dark.

JANNA: Hello? Oh swell. We still got a dial tone, though. Anybody you want to call while we still got a dial tone?

ANTONY: *(Holds his head)* Oh no, oh no, oh no, oh no.

JANNA: *(To* ANTONY*)* What?

(ANTONY *continues oh no-ing in a low monotone.* JANNA *hangs up the telephone.)*

JANNA: Antony? Antony stop saying oh no and tell me what's wrong.

ANTONY: Hit me.

JANNA: Hit—?

ANTONY: Hit me, knock me out. Hit me and knock me out. *(Panting)*

JANNA: I'm sorry, but I seem to be missing a crucial piece of information here.

ANTONY: I can't stand it. I can't stand it.

JANNA: Are you sick? Is there some medicine? Nitroglycerine? Antony, talk to me.

(ANTONY *crosses to a wall, loosening his shirt collar, moaning "no." A desperate person)*

JANNA: What? What is it? *(Dials)* Okay, okay. Take it easy, I'm calling 9-1-1. Answer. Come on, answer, pick up the phone. *(The phone goes dead, she depresses the dialtone button several times.)* Oh great. Oh, just great. *(Hangs up)*

ANTONY: *(Moaning)* No no no no no no no. *(Continues)*

(JANNA *watches* ANTONY *for a minute, then speaks slowly and distinctly with great calm.)*

JANNA: Okay, Son, come on, you gotta help me here. Just lift up your head. Come on, give it a try.

(ANTONY *tries.)*

JANNA: Okay, good. Okay, Antony, look in my face. Focus on my face.

(ANTONY *does.)*

JANNA: You're not breathing, son, that will not help.

(ANTONY *breathes and looks away.*)

JANNA: No, look at me. *(Joking)* You have to look and breathe at the same time. Come on. Look at me and breathe.

(ANTONY *breathes and looks at* JANNA.)

JANNA: There's nothing to be afraid about. Do you want me to get you some water?

ANTONY: I don't know I don't know.

JANNA: How about an aspirin?

ANTONY: *(Hysterical giggle)*

JANNA: Yeah, I guess you need stuff I don't happen to carry.

(ANTONY *starts to spin out again.*)

JANNA: No no, come on back, you had a little laugh, that's a good start. Look at me.

(ANTONY *does, to distract him.*)

JANNA: Let me tell you about the girls. Boy, I wonder what they're doing. How they're coping. Boy, I sure hope the power's not out at school.

ANTONY: Girls.

JANNA: Lucy and Terroba. Ten and fourteen.

ANTONY: *(Trying)* Terroba… *(Breathes)*

JANNA: Yeah, she hates her name. She's a great kid. Lucy is a horrible kid. Lucy is mean.

(ANTONY *takes several deep breaths.*)

JANNA: Now come on! I just told you my kid is mean. Respond, man.

ANTONY: *(Trying)* …Lucy is mean.

JANNA: Hey, I get to say she's mean, you don't get to say she's mean.

ANTONY: Please—

JANNA: …Okay. I say be generous, give back to the community. She says what'd the community ever give me. Whatever I ask, there's a fuss. She has no friends, and if you believe her, she doesn't care. The angriest ten-year-old in America. *(Realizes)* Is this what that was about before? Fire safety? The doors to the stairwell?

(ANTONY nods.)

JANNA: You want an office without an elevator.

(ANTONY nods.)

JANNA: *(Realizes)* Yeah, you thought you'd be working in that converted old Victorian. Getting stuck with this rickety old elevator must have been quite a shock.

ANTONY: Oh! *(Gasps, chokes, pants)*

(JANNA studies ANTONY for a minute. She shifts tactics.)

JANNA: How did you hide this from those Wall Street guys?

ANTONY: *(Pants)* I don't know.

JANNA: If they knew, they wouldn't let it alone.

ANTONY: No.

JANNA: Always on the lookout for any weakness—

ANTONY: Flaw.

JANNA: And once they see it…

ANTONY: Yeah…

JANNA: They never let you forget it.

ANTONY: Never.

JANNA: Force you into the saunas with the guys.

ANTONY: Not saunas—

JANNA: No, I've seen them.

ANTONY: Steam.

JANNA: Oh yeah, steam rooms. Naked men, shoulder to shoulder flexing their muscles.

ANTONY: Bad.

JANNA: Make you take the tiny corporate jet.

ANTONY: Say it's a special privilege!

JANNA: Yeah, watch to see if it makes you squirm.

ANTONY: Mustn't squirm. Once you squirm, they don't let up. They put little sticks on the fire, throw in the logs, burn down the whole house, get ready to roast the pig.

JANNA: Start to play little games on you.

ANTONY: Little!

JANNA: Stop the elevator mid-floor.

ANTONY: Block the exit door.

JANNA: Light a cigarette.

ANTONY: Any defect, any weakness. Allergic to cigarettes? Take you to a bar. Engaged to be married? Get you a call girl. Trying to save some money? Make you join *the club*—hand you the card of their *tailor*—walk you by the Porsche showroom—and the young guys are the worst.

JANNA: Uh huh.

ANTONY: *(Over)* They took me jogging, but it wasn't a jog, it was a race. We were flying from the get-go. If anybody has a problem, he doesn't show it. We're in a row, me in the middle. We come to a hill, it's steep, but I feel good, I want to pick up the pace. Not much, but it's a hill so not much is a lot. I feel something tickling the hairs of my arms. The guys are crowding me, close enough that I feel them with the hairs on my arms. Then, it's not just the hairs on my arms, but my skin can feel these guys, and they're not just tapping me on the shoulder, they're squeezing me, they're pushing against me. I try to get ahead, but they're squeezing me. I turn my head to the left to tell this guy to give me some room, and he's wearing headphones and blinders. I turn to my right, and shout "hey, hey, give me some space." And this guy turns his head he's grinning, grinning like his face is going to split. Grinning and jogging. I start running, really running, a sprint, I'm all squeezed together and running in a sprint. Not only do they keep up, they run faster, they run faster than they've ever run. They're running to beat the band, and it's all I can do to keep up. Uphill, squeezed together, running to beat the band. I got to get away. I can't go to the left, I can't go to the right. The only thing I can do is fall behind. I won't do that. I won't go slower than everybody else. I'll fall down dead in the road before I'll go slower than everybody else. What are you smiling about?

JANNA: Doctor Freud, at your service.

ANTONY: What?

JANNA: I read it. Somebody's in a panic, you make them talk about something worse.

ANTONY: *(Realizes)* Oh. *(Brief pause, he looks around.)* I'm not...I'm okay.

(JANNA checks the phone.)

JANNA: Dead.

(Brief pause. ANTONY is embarrassed.)

ANTONY: I couldn't stand them.

JANNA: I see them in court.

ANTONY: But I was becoming just like them.

JANNA: Unavoidable, I guess.

ANTONY: I had to get away. Reinvent myself.

JANNA: Free-range chicken?

ANTONY: It's a start.

(Brief pause)

JANNA: *(To break the silence)* What kind of law were you doing?

ANTONY: We called it environmental consulting.

JANNA: Helping clients skirt the E P A?

ANTONY: *(Nods)* Loopholes. Looking for loopholes.

JANNA: *We're* looking for loopholes.

ANTONY: Yes, but we're plugging them up.

(Pause. ANTONY and JANNA are both embarrassed by the silence.)

ANTONY: Thanks... *(Brief pause)* I'm sorry. I'm really really sorry.

JANNA: Don't worry about it.

ANTONY: You've done a really good job on uh India.

JANNA: Thanks.

ANTONY: Great photographs.

JANNA: Thanks.

ANTONY: Are they real?

JANNA: Of course they're real. What do you mean, are they real?

ANTONY: Oh, I didn't know. Great.

JANNA: You thought I faked the photographs?

ANTONY: For a good cause.

(JANNA is slightly appalled, but also amused at his gall.)

JANNA: I don't fake evidence.

ANTONY: Well, not when you have it.

JANNA: I don't fake evidence. I don't jeopardize my case with faked evidence.

ANTONY: Janna, I was just—it happens, you know.

JANNA: Not here. Not this case, not this office. Man! Sam said you were a shark; I should have asked what he meant.

ANTONY: He called me a shark?

JANNA: Don't look so proud.

ANTONY: No, I'm just surprised...that he, you know, could see that in me.

JANNA: No feeding frenzy here, friend.

ANTONY: No, no I won't—

JANNA: This is law-abiding law, win or lose.

ANTONY: No, I want that, I really want that.

JANNA: Part of the new you?

(ANTONY *nods. Brief pause*)

JANNA: *(Continued)* Did you ever try to deal with the claustrophobia?

ANTONY: Oh yeah. My car has no trunk, no locks on the closets or bathroom doors, I never go in caves or mines, I meet people in restaurants instead of taking elevators to their offices—I try to cover all the bases.

JANNA: I meant...ever try to get over it. See a doctor.

ANTONY: I don't like doctors. My father's a doctor.

JANNA: A *psychiatrist*.

ANTONY: Forget it; they lock you in closets.

JANNA: They know what they're doing.

ANTONY: No, they're just guessing. It's all opinion and guesses.

JANNA: All of psychiatry is opinion and guesses?

ANTONY: All of it.

JANNA: The math, the chemistry, biology, genetics, behavioral statistics?

ANTONY: I didn't say they weren't *educated* guesses.

JANNA: *Very* educated. I was going to be a psychiatrist.

ANTONY: I didn't know that.

JANNA: Why should you know that?

ANTONY: No—I shouldn't—

JANNA: What? Is there some file you get to look at before you come work for me? Read all about how I didn't go to medical school?

ANTONY: No! It's just an interesting thing to know—and I did it...did it *didn't*...know it. *(Scuffling)* Medical school is a lot of school. Even more than law.

JANNA: Eight years.

ANTONY: Now I'm gonna all the time be thinking you're psychoanalyzing me.

JANNA: I didn't like it, Antony.

ANTONY: Every time you look at me, I'm just going to wonder.

JANNA: I'm not interested.

ANTONY: People are interesting, their personalities.

JANNA: Don't flatter yourself.

ANTONY: *(Brief pause, then sighs)*

JANNA: I'm sorry.

ANTONY: About what?

JANNA: I didn't mean you personally aren't interesting.

ANTONY: Oh, I'm not insulted. I'm exhausted.

JANNA: Me, too.

ANTONY: That was intense.

JANNA: *(Joking)* Yeah, I could really use a cigarette.

ANTONY: Oh, please don't.

JANNA: I—it was a joke.

ANTONY: A joke?

JANNA: A little joke. A tiny one. Never mind.

ANTONY: I didn't hear a joke. *(Figures it out)* Oh! Like after sex a cigarette. *(Babble)* Oh. Yes, you're right… very intense. But not very sexy, I mean, it wasn't, I certainly didn't mean for it uh to be, it was an accident, it's not professional and I wouldn't—

JANNA: It was just a joke, Antony.

ANTONY: Um…I used to smoke.

JANNA: Yeah, me, too. Until I found Lucy with a pack.

ANTONY: The one who's ten?

JANNA: She's ten. She smokes.

ANTONY: I wasn't allowed to smoke until I was sixteen.

JANNA: You were allowed? Your parents allowed you?

ANTONY: Practically forced me. So of course I don't smoke. You should allow Lucy.

JANNA: I can't allow her, I have to stop her.

ANTONY: You could show her those lung cancer photos. Freshman biology. People were quitting in droves.

JANNA: Let's hope they still show them.

ANTONY: And that she goes to college.

JANNA: Why wouldn't she go to college?

ANTONY: Not everybody goes to college—not everybody takes biology—I don't know. *(Trying to get to a safer subject)* I don't know how I ever smoked at all.

I don't even go to clubs anymore; I can't tolerate the smoke. Especially jazz clubs.

JANNA: Why especially them?

ANTONY: There's always more smoke in jazz clubs than in rock clubs.

JANNA: That's not true; beer, cigarettes, and rock and roll.

ANTONY: The people who go to jazz clubs chain smoke.

JANNA: ...*Black* people? The black people who go to jazz clubs chain smoke?

ANTONY: *(Impassioned)* I honestly don't even know how anybody in the black community can still smoke. If they could see those horrible men they're making rich, they'd quit.

JANNA: ...The black community?

ANTONY: ...What?

JANNA: Where is this black community?

ANTONY: What are you talking about?

JANNA: Like we all live together in some African village. Have meetings in which we decide our political line. The black community. Where do you get off?

ANTONY: I am so sick of this.

JANNA: *You're* sick of it?

ANTONY: You have no idea how sick I am of triple thinking before I say anything.

JANNA: You mean this is you *thinking* before you speak?

ANTONY: It's not me thinking about what *I'm* thinking. It's me thinking about what *you're* thinking I'm thinking that's the problem. I'm not thinking anything.

JANNA: I'll say.

ANTONY: I took black studies.

JANNA: Did you pass?!

ANTONY: It is *reasonable*. It is *reasonable* to say black community. It does not imply, what you said, village. Some things are simply reasonable.

JANNA: Oh sure. "You black people", "why do all you black people", "why is it that black people—"

ANTONY: I didn't say all you black people, I didn't say you black people. I said black community. Implying—

JANNA: Implying a hot line. The black hot line. Janna finds out something in the morning and by nightfall the whole black community knows about it. "Hello, is this the black community? Would you please spread the word that Janna's new assistant took the job so he'd be working with *Fitz*?"

ANTONY: Cut me some slack.

JANNA: Just once I wish you would surprise me. Come in here, take over.

(JANNA *picks up his tattered book from the shelf.* ANTONY *takes it from her.*)

ANTONY: Give me that, that's mine.

JANNA: Act like you own the place.

ANTONY: I didn't—

JANNA: You're all the same.

ANTONY: Oh, I see. *You're* allowed to generalize.

JANNA: Why don't you just say "they" or "them"? That's what every other white person in America says. That's what's on T V for my girls to watch. Black criminals and murderers and prostitutes. "What do you wanna be when *you* grow up little black girl?"

ANTONY: (*Snapping*) Man, no wonder they stuck you over here.

JANNA: *(Snapping)* Nobody stuck me anyplace!

ANTONY: *(Snapping)* Twisting everything I say. You've snapped, Janna. Snap. Snapping at everything.

JANNA: *(Snapping)* Shut up, just shut up.

(Crack, wind, blinding light. ANTONY, *still with his book, goes into the closet.* JANNA *stands frozen on the other side of the room.)*

(Scene Two. Virginia, the past, a room in a tobacco plantation house; JAMES NAYLOR, *ten years old, child of the manor,* ANNIE, *eight years old, a slave, stands in the corner. There is no sound of wind, but sounds of summer, a golden glow from the lamps soften the light. Worried, she listens attentively for a moment and advances into the room.)*

ANNIE: *(A whisper)* James? *(Pause)* Where you at, James?

(ANNIE turns and walks to the closet, opens it. JAMES *tumbles out holding the tattered old book; he is panting from fear. He holds his face in his hands.)*

ANNIE: James, come outta there.

JAMES: *(Panting)* Annie, Annie, Annie…

ANNIE: Take you hands down.

JAMES: I gonna die. I gonna die.

ANNIE: You ain't dyin'.

JAMES: I tried to yell, nothing come out.

ANNIE: You ain't dying. I tell you you ain't. Quiet now. Whachu doin' in that closet?

JAMES: I hid out so I didn't havta go. I thought I'd be stuck in there forever.

ANNIE: I heard you in my mind. *(Exiting)*

JAMES: Where you going? Don't go.

ANNIE: I got ta take up sheets.

JAMES: You don't got ta take up sheets.

ANNIE: You ain't no bossman, James.

JAMES: Don' leave me, Annie, don't leave me 'lone.

ANNIE: You alright.

JAMES: Please, don't go. I got something. I got something to show you. I know you like it.

ANNIE: …I ain' 'lowd.

JAMES: No, it don't matter.

ANNIE: I get beat.

JAMES: She ain't here!

ANNIE: Missy Naylor gone?

JAMES: They neither one of them here.

ANNIE: Where they at?

JAMES: Ma and Pa gone, they ain't coming back.

ANNIE: She come back. She beat me.

JAMES: They ain't coming back 'til tomorrow. We can play whatever we want.

(That information is liberating.)

ANNIE: Whatchu got?

JAMES: It's a book.

ANNIE: Let me see.

JAMES: This is my book I first learned to read on.

(ANNIE *opens the book.*)

JAMES: I read harder books now, but this one is a good one to start on.

ANNIE: What's this?

JAMES: *(Reads)*
When the sun is out to stay
come back to me and we will play

a game of light
of light.

ANNIE: This is that?

JAMES: "When the sun is…"

ANNIE: "When the sun is…"

JAMES: "…out to stay." *(Points to single words. Sing-song)*
"When the sun is out to stay."

ANNIE: *(Imitating him)* "When the sun is out to stay."

JAMES: "Come back to me and we will play."

ANNIE: "Come back to me and we will play."

JAMES: "A game of light, of light."

ANNIE: "A game of light, of light." *(Fast, eyes closed)*
"When the sun is out to stay, come back to me and we
will play, a game of light, of light."

JAMES: That's it. That's reading.

ANNIE: I'm reading?

JAMES: You have to *look* at the words when you say
them. Then you reading. That's how I learned it.

ANNIE: When the sun comes out to play, come back—

JAMES: Stay. "When the sun comes out to *stay*." Each
one of these bunches of letters is a separate whole
word. This one says *when*; this one is *the*; this is *sun*.
See?

ANNIE: *(Slowly, points)* "When. The. Sun. Comes. Out.
To. Stay. Comeback—

JAMES: No. Come back is two words. *(Points)* Come.
Back.

ANNIE: Come back to me… *(Starts over)* "When the sun
comes out to stay, come back to me and we will play, a
game of light, of light."

JAMES: You practice that.

ANNIE: I will.

JAMES: Then you havta learn the rest of the pages.

ANNIE: A new one every day.

JAMES: …Yeah, you smart.

ANNIE: You read me the rest of them?

JAMES: *(Brief pause)* You don't need me to.

ANNIE: I do.

JAMES: Once you know one page, the rest is easy. You'll see. You know this page?

ANNIE: I know it.

JAMES: The rest of the ones will be easy for you.

ANNIE: I can show Neely.

JAMES: No.

ANNIE: Yes. I'll learn good so I can show him how.

JAMES: You the one's got to learn.

ANNIE: How come not Neely?

JAMES: Cause I said so.

ANNIE: Don't you like Neely?

JAMES: I like Neely fine.

ANNIE: He'll like it.

JAMES: You don't want to be showin' somebody else the book. You got to keep the book secret…or you can't have it!

ANNIE: *(Reluctant)* Alright. *(She opens the book; it makes her happy.)* What's this?

JAMES: That says James Naylor. So I know it's mine. I write better now. I'll write your name in it.

ANNIE: My name?

JAMES: So you know it's yours.

ANNIE: *(Surprised)* It's mine?

JAMES: Yes. You take it, you learn to read on it. Use it to practice writin'. *(He gets a pen from the table.)* I'll cross out my name. *(Writes)* A-N-N-I-E. Annie.

ANNIE: My name.

JAMES: You do it.

ANNIE: *(She tries, she likes it.)* My name.

JAMES: That's good. You gonna practice so you can write me letters.

ANNIE: You goin' some place?

JAMES: I—I ain't. *(Brief pause)* Promise me you'll learn it.

ANNIE: You Mama find out, she hit me.

JAMES: She ain't gonna find out. *(Takes paper, writes)* Here. At the end of you letter, you write this: "sincerely, your good friend, Annie."

ANNIE: I can't write all that.

JAMES: Yes. Just one letter at a time, you can do it.

ANNIE: I got ink on me. My Mama's gonna know I was in the pens.

JAMES: She won't see it. Look. It just blends right away on you.

ANNIE: It don't. Pen mark, right here. Let's play with that. *(She points to microscope.)*

JAMES: I want you to practice writin'.

ANNIE: That you look at with your Pa.

JAMES: ...Nobody's 'lowd to touch that.

ANNIE: They gone.

JAMES: Pa says the best way to get something broke is to let other people go touching it.

ANNIE: He let you.

JAMES: A whole year he wouldn't. But now I can because I'm ten.

ANNIE: You ten?

JAMES: I am. When you ten, you get to do stuff.

ANNIE: Why?

JAMES: 'Cause you on your way to being grown. Ten is the first time you is two numbers. Then you's two numbers 'til you die. Nobody gets to three numbers.

ANNIE: Am I two numbers?

JAMES: No. You eight. Eight's one number.

ANNIE: Do I have to wait 'til I'm two numbers?

JAMES: For what?

ANNIE: To look inside this. *(Microscope)*

(A brief pause. JAMES realizes ANNIE won't be there when she's two numbers.)

JAMES: *(With resolve)* No. No I changed my mind. You don't havta wait 'til you ten. You can look at it today. You can look at it right now. You can look at it all you want.

(JAMES gets it down, ANNIE touches it, she wipes it off.)

JAMES: Careful.

ANNIE: I'm just wipin' it.

JAMES: It ain't a ornament, Annie. It's a scientific tool.

ANNIE: What do I do?

JAMES: Look down this.

(ANNIE does. She looks away, sad, tears.)

ANNIE: I can't do it. I can't.

JAMES: What's the matter wi'chu?

ANNIE: I ain't two numbers.

JAMES: Stop cryin'. What's wrong?

ANNIE: I can't see nothing.

JAMES: There ain't nothing there! You got to put something there to see. *(He takes slide from a box, pokes the tip of his finger, and squeezes a drop of blood onto the slide. He puts the slide carefully under the scope, looks, adjusts.)* Whachu carrying on like that! Don't be crying like that. You can see it good as anybody, soon's somethin's on it. There. Take a look now.

ANNIE: *(Excited)* What is it?

JAMES: It's blood. That's what blood looks like from the inside.

ANNIE: …It's alive. *(Excited, extends her finger)* Do me.

(JAMES pokes her finger, puts drop of blood on slide. ANNIE looks.)

ANNIE: Is that what you look at all the time? Blood?

JAMES: Not just blood. Put a drop of water from the well, you get to see all the little things livin' in it. Put a drop of water from the creek, everything's different.

ANNIE: Why?

JAMES: That's science.

ANNIE: *(Looks)* My blood. *(Touches microscope)* Science.

JAMES: No, Annie, this a *microscope*. It's a tool so I can *learn* science.

ANNIE: I want to learn science.

JAMES: You don't have one of these.

ANNIE: I'll get one.

JAMES: It cost two thousand dollars.

ANNIE: …Is that more than five hundred?

JAMES: It's a sight more.

ANNIE: Bonny say he a five-hundred-dollar slave.

JAMES: *(He puts his slide back on and looks.)* Yeah, well, this here microscope is equal to *four* five-hundred-dollar slaves. These slides cost five dollars each. So don't break one or I have to pay for it.

ANNIE: Let me look again. *(She does.)* My blood is alive.

JAMES: That's *my* blood.

ANNIE: It look like mine.

JAMES: Let me see. *(Looks at both)* That can't be—oh, I know why they look the same. You got Pa's blood inside you.

ANNIE: *(Brief pause)* How Masta Naylor's blood get inside me?

JAMES: It's a secret.

ANNIE: How come you get to know it?

JAMES: I reckon 'cause I turned ten.

ANNIE: Can I know when I turned ten?

JAMES: *(Brief pause, sad)* Oh, Annie, I'm sorry. *(He hugs her)* Promise me you write me a letter. You havta write to me. I'll die if you don't write me a letter.

(ANNIE is astonished by the hug. The sound of wind rising as the lights change to storm. Scene Three. The present, ANTONY, JANNA, the wind, pale daylight. He hugs her as JAMES hugged ANNIE—a needy hug.)

JANNA: Antony—are you—?

ANTONY: *(Breaking away)* I'm sorry I'm sorry. *(Panting)*

JANNA: Hey, come on. Don't go there again, I can't take it.

ANTONY: *(Little laugh)* No, I'm— *(Deep breath)* I'm okay. I'll be okay.

JANNA: Just keep breathing. *(She looks around, trying to figure out what happened. She gets her coat out of the closet and stuffs it under the door.)*

ANTONY: Use mine, too.

(JANNA does. She touches her microscope.)

JANNA: Did you move this?

ANTONY: No.

JANNA: *(Joking)* Maybe it was the wind.

ANTONY: *(Little laugh)* Yeah. *(Brief pause, trying)* Was that for medical school?

JANNA: *(Snapping)* It's an antique!

ANTONY: I didn't know. How am I supposed to know—? There's a box of slides—looks all ready for research to me.

JANNA: The slides are antiques, too. *(Brief pause)* I didn't mean to snap at you.

ANTONY: That's okay, I'm an idiot about antiques.

JANNA: *(Snapping)* Before! I didn't mean to snap at you before!

ANTONY: ...Did you mean to snap at me now? Did you mean to snap at me about the microscope? Did you mean to snap at me—

JANNA: *(Snapping)* I'm not snapping at you!

ANTONY: Snapping one minute, joking the next. I can't keep up.

JANNA: You're a New Yorker, you're supposed to keep up. *(She smiles)* Nobody stuck me here, Antony.

ANTONY: What?

JANNA: You said "no wonder they stuck you here." Before...when I snapped at you.

ANTONY: I didn't mean to say that.

JANNA: Fitz tell you that? That they stuck me here?

ANTONY: ...No.

JANNA: *(Setting the record straight)* I did this. I found this office, I called the movers, I put myself here. And E D E has to foot the bill until Fitz is gone. The second he's gone, I'm out of this building, back at my sweet little desk. In the Sweet Little Victorian.

ANTONY: What if Fitz doesn't go?

JANNA: Then I'll go public and let the courts fix him.

ANTONY: It's been over five months—

JANNA: I have everybody's support. *(Joking)* Now don't you go worrying about me, Son. He'll go. He can't stall much longer. He'll be gone from Pike Street, and you and me get to go back.

(ANTONY walks around. He takes his tattered book back to the shelf.)

ANTONY: Um—

JANNA: Please—I was out of line. Go ahead, anything you want, really.

(ANTONY puts his book on the shelf. He picks up the photo of Lucy and Terroba.)

ANTONY: This little one...she is so—

JANNA: Yeah, their Dad was dark.

ANTONY: ...I wasn't going to say that. I was—I was just going to say that she doesn't look like she could have a mean bone in her body, that's all I was going to say.

JANNA: That's because she's with Terroba. When she's with Terroba she's all sugar...angel food cake. With me or anybody else, she's a bitter lemon. A lot of people comment on how dark she is.

ANTONY: Not white people.

JANNA: *(Joking)* No. For white people black is black regardless.

ANTONY: That's not what I meant.

JANNA: Yeah, we black folks know better. We got color charts.

ANTONY: *(Brief pause)* I think I'm in the middle of a snap, and it turns out I'm in the middle of a joke.

JANNA: Terroba takes after my family. We got a lotta light in my family. Robert was dark. Lucy takes after Robert.

ANTONY: *(Brief pause)* Sam told me what happened to your husband. I'm sorry.

JANNA: Why'd he do that?

ANTONY: I don't know.

JANNA: What? Was he just *filling you in?* Explaining how it is I have two kids and no man?

ANTONY: It wasn't like that—

JANNA: So you wouldn't go thinking I was an unmarried black woman with two chillun—?

ANTONY: He was looking out for you.

JANNA: Even a dead husband is better than no husband?

(Brief pause)

ANTONY: I can't tell if you're snapping or joking.

JANNA: You need the advanced course. Black Studies 1-0-2 is black humor.

ANTONY: I thought 1-0-2 was black magic.

JANNA: *(Snorts at his joke)* You wouldn't have been allowed in the class in my day.

ANTONY: In black magic?

JANNA: In black studies. No white students allowed.

ANTONY: Why would you want that?

JANNA: To have a place to speak freely.

ANTONY: You can speak freely.

JANNA: Not when the room is full of white strangers. When the room is full of white strangers you worry about what you say.

ANTONY: When the room is full of black strangers you worry, too.

JANNA: Not about getting lynched you don't.

ANTONY: Like there's no racial violence against white people.

JANNA: Yeah, racism is really hard on white people.

(Brief pause)

ANTONY: It is when three black kids beat me up and don't even take my money.

JANNA: …I don't think the white kids who chased me into my house were looking for money.

ANTONY: …It wasn't an artist who spray-painted "white man equals dead man" on my car.

JANNA: Maybe about the same time somebody was burning a cross on my parents' lawn?

ANTONY: The Congressional Black Caucus wouldn't give me a job interview. The N A A C P would rather I donate money than serve on a committee.

JANNA: The wife of our esteemed comrade Fitz ran up to me at the Christmas party and asked me for a *corn bread* recipe. *(Brief pause)* The last time I went to a play, some lady in the bathroom handed me a quarter and said, "please bring me a towel, dear". Last year, the oncoming chairman of our board asked me to see to the urinals in the men's room. Come on, Antony, come on. What's the matter with you? Give me your best shot. I'm just getting started here.

ANTONY: ...I did that.

JANNA: What? You did what?

ANTONY: What you said, the corn bread.

JANNA: You did not ask a black woman for a corn bread recipe.

ANTONY: I met a guy at a party. I started talking about the Knicks.

JANNA: A black guy?

(ANTONY *nods.*)

JANNA: What did he say?

ANTONY: He didn't know anything about the Knicks. I didn't know anything about the Knicks. It was a pretty short conversation. *(Pause)* So you want to arm wrestle or something?

JANNA: Why, so you can win?

ANTONY: Yeah. What did you do with the quarter?

JANNA: What quarter?

ANTONY: The one from the bathroom.

JANNA: *(Snorts a laugh)* I called the girls, told them I loved them. That's what I do when it gets funky.

(Brief pause. He is weary. He sighs.)

ANTONY: *(Joking)* Boy, I could really use a cigarette.

JANNA: Can't help ya—all us black folks done give 'em up.

ANTONY: ...Listen—what I meant before—*before*, when I was talking about smoking. And...um—

JANNA: The black community.

ANTONY: And hot line!

JANNA: And hot line.

ANTONY: Those guys, those tobacco guys were always coming up from Virginia and staying at our apartment. I saw them up close. All I meant was if you saw them up close you wouldn't buy cigarettes from them. That's all I meant.

JANNA: What were they doing at your apartment?

ANTONY: Conferring on a major level.

JANNA: With who?

ANTONY: My father.

JANNA: ...You said your Dad's a doctor.

ANTONY: He is. He's also a "research consultant".

JANNA: How can he *do* that?

ANTONY: He *smokes*. It gives him a certain moral stature.

JANNA: Well, now I really respect him.

ANTONY: "Why if it weren't for smokers, the dry cleaners in this country would go out of business."

JANNA: He says that?

ANTONY: A direct quote.

JANNA: What do you say to him?

ANTONY: I don't talk to him. I haven't talked to him since my mother's funeral. Almost two years.

JANNA: Does he know you're in Seattle?

ANTONY: *(Happy)* No.

JANNA: You can't cut him off like that. You need your dad.

ANTONY: For what?

JANNA: If something comes up—if there's trouble.

ANTONY: He'd be the first one to jump ship.

JANNA: No. Dads have to go down with the ship, it's the law of the sea.

ANTONY: You don't know this man.

JANNA: You can't cut off your dad. You need your dad.

ANTONY: I'm doing just fine with no "dad."

JANNA: You're not doing fine.

ANTONY: In what way am I not doing fine?

JANNA: Antony, you were screaming for me to hit you and knock you out.

ANTONY: I got a job, didn't I? A job nobody had to get *for* me. Nobody made *a call*. I'm not stuck below the *"seventy-five-thousand dollar ceiling"*! I have a place to live and a car to drive. I'm doing fine.

JANNA: *(Brief pause)* Oh, worse and worse.

ANTONY: What?

JANNA: *(Amazed)* Let's see. More than seventy-five is at least seventy-six. Now I don't want you to think I'm a litigious type of person, but when my company sends me an assistant and pays him ten grand more than me, that certainly is sounding actionable.

ANTONY: I went to Yale.

JANNA: Ta ra ra boom de ay.

ANTONY: Do you have any idea what my classmates are making?

JANNA: Almost as much as my classmates. My Harvard classmates.

ANTONY: Harvard *Law*?

JANNA: Harvard Law. *(Brief pause, sigh)* Law Review.

ANTONY: You made Law Review?

JANNA: Yes, and affirmative action did not get me Law Review, no matter what you're thinking about how I got into Harvard.

ANTONY: Please don't tell me what I'm thinking.

JANNA: *(Containing herself)* Fair enough. I won't tell you what you're thinking. I'll tell you what I'm thinking.

ANTONY: Janna, please—

JANNA: I'm thinking ... we should talk about your salary.

ANTONY: I don't want to talk about my salary.

JANNA: I'll bet you don't.

ANTONY: I'm not even supposed to. It's in my contract.

JANNA: Then let's talk about *my* salary.

ANTONY: Your salary has nothing to do with me.

JANNA: If we're going to work together, you have to understand me on this—

ANTONY: This simply is none of my business.

JANNA: I've been at E D E for five years, five—

ANTONY: No! I don't want to hear about it. I won't listen to you.

(ANTONY turns away. JANNA watches him in disbelief. He won't look at her. A brief pause.)

ANTONY: *(Contained fury)* Oh please. Please don't do that.

JANNA: Don't do what?

ANTONY: My name's *Antony*.

JANNA: *(Confused)* What?

ANTONY: Don't call me Tony. You really mustn't call me Tony.

JANNA: I didn't call you Tony.

ANTONY: I heard you. "Tony Tony Tony, you have to hear me out, you just have to."

JANNA: *(Amazed)* I didn't say it.

ANTONY: Listen to me Janna, it's not my fault how much they pay me.

JANNA: *(Pause, tries to gain some control of herself and the situation)* Alright. Alright, Antony. You're right. It isn't. You are not the person with whom I should take up this matter. I shall take up this matter with Sam.

ANTONY: Fine. Take it up with Sam.

JANNA: I will.

ANTONY: I'm sure…it's just an oversight.

JANNA: Sure.

ANTONY: Bookkeeping…

JANNA: Yeah, he wouldn't do that.

ANTONY: He's a good guy.

JANNA: Good guy? Well, that's the understatement of the century.

ANTONY: Sam's a good guy. He's not Jesus Christ, for pete's sake.

JANNA: You think somebody on Wall Street lets you bring your kids to work?

ANTONY: I don't have kids.

JANNA: Bring-your-daughters-to-work day…for a year?

ANTONY: When was that?

JANNA: When we first got here.

ANTONY: I didn't know he did that.

JANNA: I couldn't let them out of my sight.

ANTONY: And they were just…there? In the office?

JANNA: I stuck them in a corner with toys.

ANTONY: A year?

JANNA: A lot of different toys.

ANTONY: God, I'm glad you got over that.

JANNA: When did I say I was over it? I'm not over it. Terroba wants to go for a ride with the older kids, I say no. She's the best kid a mother could have, I say no, no you can't. You can't go in a car, you can't go to a party, you can't go to school with your friends, you can't have a leather jacket. I won't let her own a leather jacket, her heart is broken.

ANTONY: You don't let her go to school?

JANNA: She goes to school. She just doesn't go with her friends.

ANTONY: Why not?

JANNA: She goes to private school. That's what they're wearing in the picture. Their uniforms.

ANTONY: They both go to private school?

JANNA: You don't think they'd wear those outfits on purpose?

ANTONY: Huh.

JANNA: What?

ANTONY: No, nothing, I didn't know.

JANNA: Man, it's amazing anybody gets any work done over there on Pike Street.

ANTONY: Janna, we don't sit around the office talking about you—I just thought they went to public school.

JANNA: Why should you think that?

ANTONY: You're the one talking about being generous.

JANNA: My kids can't go to private school?

ANTONY: I'm just trying to make some sense out of it.

JANNA: It makes perfectly good sense to me.

ANTONY: You want your kid to be generous. Your... Lucy. You want her to give back to the community—giving back to the community is not private school.

JANNA: Do you have any idea what I have to sacrifice so they can go to private school?

ANTONY: If they went to the public school, you'd put more effort into making the schools better.

JANNA: I should sacrifice my kids for the greater good?

ANTONY: No, you just want somebody else to do it.

JANNA: I'm taking care of my kids.

ANTONY: It's selfish.

JANNA: What is?

ANTONY: I think you have a tendency to be selfish.

JANNA: You know me under a week I have a tendency?

ANTONY: You look after yourself.

JANNA: I take care of my kids.

ANTONY: At the expense of others. The Fitz thing is selfish.

JANNA: *(Amazed, pause)* You're right, Antony. It *is* selfish. If I were *un*selfish, I'd demand a trial to show the whole world the true Fitz. But I'm too selfish to do that to myself. Fitz is getting off easy because I am *selfish.*

ANTONY: You're making him leave E D E.

JANNA: Pity. He's going to have to go into the marketplace and work for mere millions now. He's getting off easy.

ANTONY: You could look for another way.

JANNA: Are you suggesting that I quit?

ANTONY: No!

JANNA: Well, what is this "other way"?

ANTONY: He's not there three weeks out of four as it is.

JANNA: I don't want him around me for a second.

ANTONY: We could figure out a schedule.

JANNA: And I wonder who'd get the ass end of that deal.

ANTONY: You could give a deposition. Put it on file. If Fitz so much as looks at you, he's out on his behind. With censure.

JANNA: I gave a deposition.

ANTONY: ...No.

JANNA: Yes. So did Fitz.

ANTONY: I didn't know—

JANNA: We'll just add it to the ever-growing list of the things you don't know.

ANTONY: Sam didn't tell me— What do they say?

JANNA: Mine says what happened. Fitz states that he never laid a hand on me. Then five minutes into his tape he blames his behavior on how I dress.

ANTONY: *(Brief pause)* He accused you of provoking an incident that he says didn't happen?

JANNA: And the depositions from the other women.

ANTONY: What other women?

JANNA: The other women. Not all of them, of course. Many, many would not testify. *(Brief pause)* They are getting very selective memory over on Pike Street.

ANTONY: How could they do this to me?

JANNA: Sharks everywhere, it seems.

ANTONY: Those bastards.

JANNA: What?

ANTONY: "She's blown it all out of proportion."

JANNA: Who said that?

ANTONY: "Come on Son, do you really think Fitz would do something like that?"

JANNA: Antony—

ANTONY: It's supposed to be different here!

JANNA: *(Brief pause)* What are you talking about?

(Pause. ANTONY regains some control of himself.)

JANNA: What's going on?

ANTONY: *(Pause)* We're going to get the logging legislation.

JANNA: When hell freezes over.

ANTONY: No. It's coming out of committee.

JANNA: Since when?

ANTONY: Since the fishing lobby got involved.

JANNA: Oh. For a minute I got all giddy, thinking we'd won some environmental legislation on its merit.

ANTONY: It's going to be close, but it should pass.

JANNA: So the bill I wrote is out of committee, it's going to the floor. Was anyone ever going to let me know? Or was I going to have to read about it in the Sunday paper?

ANTONY: We were going to let you know—we just…

JANNA: What what what?! Just tell me, please.

ANTONY: Fitz isn't going to leave.

JANNA: No. He leaves, no trial. He doesn't leave, I call a lawyer. That's the deal.

ANTONY: They think you'll change your mind.

JANNA: …I won't.

ANTONY: We don't want you to take him to court.

JANNA: Who doesn't want me to?

ANTONY: The board.

JANNA: No.

ANTONY: Your good friend Sam.

JANNA: Sam supports me. The board supports me.

ANTONY: Not any more. *(Brief pause)* If you take Fitz to court, the timber lobby turns his trial into a circus. A delay in Congress, the wind shifts, we lose a vote in November what was a sure thing in May.

(A brief pause)

JANNA: *(Realizes, extreme disbelief, she is bowled over.)* … He *sent* you. He sent you.

ANTONY: And it's not just the logging vote, Janna.

JANNA: *(Betrayal, lost)* Sam.

ANTONY: It's money.

JANNA: *(Over)* Of course you make more money than me. You're not my assistant. You're my spy. Sam is a blackmailer and you're a spy.

ANTONY: I know it may sound like blackmail.

JANNA: Sounds like blackmail, is blackmail.

ANTONY: We're concerned we'll lose donations from women and women's groups.

JANNA: When did you get so down with everybody, *"We're* concerned. *We* don't want you to go to court. *We* were going to tell you." This just kills me. I've worked here five years. *You* know them four months and already you're one of the boys, somebody they can all count on. Sam. Sends you over here on a little mission.

ANTONY: I can't help how people are.

JANNA: And why should you? Why should you change a thing when it all works so well for you.

ANTONY: This isn't working for me. I didn't want this. How can you say this is working for me?

JANNA: You white man.

ANTONY: I'm fucked here.

JANNA: The tight white club.

ANTONY: Jesus Christ.

(A crack, wind, blinding light. Scene Four. ANNIE *and* JAMES, *windless, sunny, Virginia.)*

ANNIE: Why you talkin' about a letter? I can't write no letter.

JAMES: You gonna learn, that's all I mean.

ANNIE: *(Suspicious)* Where your Papa and Mama go?

JAMES: Up to Ma's family in Richmond.

ANNIE: Is it a party?

JAMES: ...It ain't no party.

ANNIE: Is somebody sick?

JAMES: No. They ain't sick.

ANNIE: Why they go?

JAMES: ...They gone...'cause Ma said something had to get done. She wants it done before she gets back.

ANNIE: What is it? *(Silence)* Do I have to do it?

JAMES: Shut up about it. I don't wanna talk about it.

ANNIE: *(Brief pause, to get even)* I *like* Missy Naylor to be gone.

JAMES: I know you do. *(To change subject)* Come on, Annie, copy down those letters in the book. You havta practice writing.

ANNIE: Missy Naylor slap me.

JAMES: She don't mean to.

ANNIE: Then why she do it?

JAMES: She don't like that Pa's nice to you.

ANNIE: She don't slap Neely. He's nice to Neely.

JAMES: Neely's dark. Ma likes slaves to look dark. She don't like them to look light. She says it ain't right for slaves to look light.

ANNIE: She slap Mama. Mama's dark as Neely.

JAMES: …Your Mama sasses.

ANNIE: She don't.

JAMES: *(Brief pause, truth)* Causa Pa. That's why.

ANNIE: She mean.

JAMES: She ain't. Don't talk about it.

ANNIE: She follows me 'round.

JAMES: Let me see you write something, Annie.

(ANNIE *puts the paper and pens back on the table. Stands away from them)*

JAMES: What you doin'?

ANNIE: Missy Naylor come to the quarter. She find everything.

JAMES: She won't.

ANNIE: She find that pie. She beat Mama.

JAMES: You should have told I *give* it to you.

ANNIE: *You* shoulda tol'. I won't take the pens.

JAMES: You have to. They you presents, they presents, they presents for you ninth birthday and you tenth birthday all you birthdays to come. All at once. You get it all at once.

ANNIE: She find the pens. She always do find what you give me.

JAMES: She ain't gonna find nothin' 'cause you ain't gonna be there.

(ANNIE *gets worried.*)

JAMES: And your paper and your pens and your book ain't gonna be there neither. Now take 'em.

ANNIE: Where I gonna be?

JAMES: You goin' away.

ANNIE: *(Scared)* Why?

JAMES: You jus' are.

ANNIE: Like Sara?

JAMES: No. Pa forbid you get sold.

ANNIE: *(Panic)* Don't send me don't send me don't send me *(Continues over* JAMES)

JAMES: Annie, Annie it's alright girl. It's alright. Don't be scared. It's alright.

ANNIE: You can't send me, James, you can't. Who gonna find you, you get stuck again? Nobody can find you but me.

JAMES: Don't say that.

ANNIE: Nobody could find you or hear you or know where you was—I heard you in my heart crying in that well—

JAMES: It ain't gonna happen again.

ANNIE: —and I listened to my heart and I found you out. I saved you.

JAMES: I called out to you in my mind.

ANNIE: And I heard you. You would have died. But I knew where you was because I heard you inside my heart. Who gonna find you you get stuck again?

JAMES: I ain't gonna get stuck again.

ANNIE: I always hear you in my mind.

JAMES: I always hear you, too.

ANNIE: Don't send me off.

JAMES: Ma wants you gone. She wants you and you Mama outta here. Tobias takin' you.

ANNIE: Where we goin?

JAMES: You going to New York.

ANNIE: ...New York in the North?

JAMES: New York City. Pa got a cousin there. Tobias will ride with you past Washington. Pa give you Mama a packet of money in her bundle. So you can buy food and all.

ANNIE: *(Afraid)* Mama know?

JAMES: She know now, I reckon.

ANNIE: When we goin'?

JAMES: You gotta be gone before Ma and Pa gets back.

ANNIE: Neely goin'?

JAMES: Neely ain't goin'.

ANNIE: I want Neely, I want him.

JAMES: Just you and you Mama.

ANNIE: *You* goin?

JAMES: Annie, I can't go.

ANNIE: ...I can't go.

JAMES: You have to. If you don't—It's you only chance.

ANNIE: ...I want...I want...I want I want *(Panting)*

JAMES: Hey, girl, don't cry. Whachu want?

ANNIE: I want I want I want I want I want I want *(Continues)*

JAMES: I can't go along.

ANNIE: I want I want I want I want, I want something I want it, I want it I want it. Please. I want it.

JAMES: I don't know…here, take this. Just take it, here, take it, hold it tight. It's yours forever and ever.

(JAMES *jams the microscope into her arms.* ANNIE *clutches it as if it were comforting; she continues to pant, panic, no words.*)

JAMES: Here, take your book along, too. *(Forces these things into her arms)* And the paper and the pens. I'll wrap it up for you in a bundle, so it'll be safe, so it don't look like nothing. You gonna write to me, won'tcha, Annie? When you learn how, you'll write me a letter won'tcha? You tell me how you are. I got to know how you are. It won't be so bad if I just can know how you are. Annie?

(The sound of wind brings us back to Seattle and the windy present, pale daylight. Scene Five. ANTONY *fusses around with the window and door a bit.* JANNA *clutches the book and microscope. She is distraught, crying.)*

ANTONY: Janna? Are you okay? Janna? Are you alright? The wind—I don't know—

JANNA: It's all a lie. Doesn't matter what anybody says, they just lying. "We don't make much money at E D E Janna, but we're honest here, we're not cutthroat, we're making the world better for your girls. You get to leave your girls a better world to live in. Your husband would be so proud. You just let Sam take care of Fitz. Sam won't let Fitz get away with it. This is not like New York, New York where they shoot you for your jacket, kill you for your jacket." They shot Robert for his *jacket*. Did *Sam* tell you that? How did he miss telling you that? Don't he know what's important at all?

ANTONY: I'm sorry, I'm sorry.

JANNA: I try to protect them. I try to raise them to be good, generous, selfless little girls. Why? Why try? Why try anything at all? Why not just dig in? Snap. Snap! Too many snaps in a row and I'll snap, I will snap. (*Pause. She pulls herself together. Puts down microscope and book.*) I seem to have torn your book.

ANTONY: It's okay, it's old.

JANNA: (*Snorts*) When is anything ever going to change?

ANTONY: Listen, Sam set me up, too.

JANNA: Why didn't he just ask me?

ANTONY: I don't know, I don't know anything.

JANNA: What did he say?

ANTONY: ...That he didn't know how you'd react—that nobody knows Janna.

JANNA: If they don't know me it's their fault.

ANTONY: You don't have anybody over, you don't go out, you eat lunch at your desk.

JANNA: If I went out to lunch, there'd be raised eyebrows over *that*.

ANTONY: Why?

JANNA: When you're black, they raise eyebrows.

ANTONY: He says you don't go to parties.

JANNA: So some wife can check my hemline? Squeeze herself between me and her husband? Act like I'm trying to steal her man, and I'm just trying to get along? I'd rather stay home and fight with Lucy!

ANTONY: Hey, *I'm* not the one says it.

JANNA: You're the one's here.

ANTONY: *(Brief pause)* Listen, when Sam was saying all this about you, he made it seem that the, the Fitz thing…

JANNA: What?

ANTONY: He made it seem like you blew it out of proportion.

JANNA: Oh, God.

ANTONY: Sam talked like he was looking out for you, for your own good.

JANNA: Sam.

ANTONY: How you'd get over it in the long run, how this was important legislation, good for the team, pesky little problem—that type of thing.

JANNA: So you felt it was fine to spy on me.

ANTONY: I didn't think of it as spying.

JANNA: That's what it is when you're looking for weaknesses. What are Janna's weaknesses—

ANTONY: I was supposed to convince you to…let it go.

JANNA: And what were you going to do after you'd passed on the prevailing wisdom? I know you have no intention of staying on as my "assistant."

ANTONY: Then…I'd go away.

JANNA: And dump India back in my lap?

ANTONY: I told Sam it had to be temporary.

JANNA: Because of the elevator? Boy, I'm sorry I missed that conversation.

ANTONY: I didn't tell him about the elevator.

JANNA: Well, what then? I mean I'm just dying of curiosity here.

ANTONY: I—I'm gonna put this right, Janna.

JANNA: What did you say to him?

ANTONY: I'm really sorry. ...I said it was—that you might accuse me...like you accused Fitz.

JANNA: Sam just let that pass? Let you say that and not defend me? Not say, "oh, that won't happen, Son. Janna won't do that." *(Brief pause)* No. He just let you think that I'm a hysterical female—making accusations at all them poor, innocent mens.

ANTONY: I had to make sure I didn't get stuck here, away from all the action. You gotta be there to know what's going down.

JANNA: That's for sure. That is for damn sure. When you're not there your colleagues forget to tell you that your legislation is going to be passed, and that your complaint is being swept under the rug, and that your assistant makes more money than you do. No. Separation is a bad idea, Antony.

ANTONY: What should we do?

JANNA: Who? You and *who*?

ANTONY: Me and you.

JANNA: ...Me and you. Man. Me and you.

ANTONY: I'm on your side, Janna.

JANNA: Too bad for my side.

ANTONY: What are we going to tell them?

JANNA: Well, I certainly wouldn't want to have to tell them that you'd spilled the beans.

ANTONY: Whatever you want—whatever you want me to say.

JANNA: What do I get?

ANTONY: What do you mean?

JANNA: If I let them keep their Fitz. What do I get?

ANTONY: …A car? Do you want a car?

JANNA: *(Snorts a laugh)* A car…! I want to go back to Pike Street.

ANTONY: Yeah, you should get that. Back to Pike Street.

JANNA: Where the action is. But then what will we do about you-know-who?

ANTONY: And, um, Fitz—goes someplace else?

JANNA: Yes, because the sight of him makes my skin crawl.

ANTONY: *(A good idea)* He can work out of here.

JANNA: Yes. Let's stick *him* in this building for a while.

(Wind hums through the building. A pause)

JANNA: *(Continued)* And one false move, let me hear about one false move out of him, let him pet a female dog and I go public, bad publicity be damned.

ANTONY: Good.

JANNA: And then there's the matter of a little salary discrepancy.

ANTONY: …It's in my contract I'm not supposed to tell other lawyers what I make.

JANNA: Well, I'd hate for you to get in trouble, Son. What do you suggest?

ANTONY: Um. *(Working it through out loud)* If your salary came to my attention…because I accidently overheard you discussing it to…your family on the telephone, I would be ethically obligated to bring the oversight to the attention of the board—who would be legally obligated to redress the discrepancy.

JANNA: From the time you were hired.

ANTONY: From the time I was hired.

JANNA: Using your salary as a base, and then increasing it with five years worth of seniority.

ANTONY: Yes.

(A brief pause. JANNA *crosses her arms.)*

ANTONY: What? What else?

JANNA: I get credit for the logging bill.

ANTONY: I don't know if—

JANNA: I want it. Tell them it's how you convinced me to forgive and forget.

ANTONY: ...Yes.

JANNA: Okay.

ANTONY: Okay? Really okay?

JANNA: Yes.

ANTONY: *(Brief pause)* Janna—um...

JANNA: What? What now?

ANTONY: It would be bad for me, if anybody at the office found out—about the panic...thing.

JANNA: Who would I tell? All my good friends?

ANTONY: It might come up.

JANNA: The only person who is going to ever know is me. And if I could unknow it, I would.

ANTONY: No, it's okay that you know.

JANNA: Because I don't count?

ANTONY: No, you count. Men are—it would be hard for me if they knew.

JANNA: They won't know from me.

(The lights come on. ANTONY *and* JANNA *are awed and relieved.)*

ANTONY: A game of light.

JANNA: Of light. Let's get out of here. *(She gets her coat and briefcase.)*

ANTONY: Hey, I'll give you a ride.

JANNA: I don't need a ride.

ANTONY: I'll give you a ride home.

JANNA: I take the bus.

ANTONY: Who knows if they're even running?

JANNA: You don't have to ride me home, Antony. Don't worry, I'll go down the elevator with you.

ANTONY: That's not why I—

JANNA: *(Sarcasm)* No? What then? You want to ride me around in your car so we can get to know each other? *(She opens the door and looks down the hall.)*

ANTONY: *(Brief pause, shakes his head)* God, it's hopeless, it's just hopeless. I think I'll just…I'm going to stay for a while. I need to do some work. Make some notes.

JANNA: Don't be ridiculous. The elevator light's on, let's go.

ANTONY: No.

JANNA: You don't want to be alone here.

ANTONY: Don't worry about it.

JANNA: If the power goes out again—

ANTONY: I'll be fine!

JANNA: Antony—

(ANTONY silences JANNA with a look. A brief moment, then she leaves. The wind hums. He puts his head in his hands. He breathes deeply to calm himself. He stands and picks up his tattered book to return it to the shelf, panting slightly. He opens it. She re-enters from the hall and stands in the open doorway.)

JANNA: *(Concerned)* Antony? Did you call me? *(Brief pause)* I heard you call me.

(ANTONY *and* JANNA *look at each other.)*

END OF PLAY

www.ingramcontent.com/pod-product-compliance
Lightning Source LLC
Chambersburg PA
CBHW070028110426
42741CB00034B/2683